Shadow
Work Journal

Copyright © 2021   Robert C. Payton

Contents

Thanks for purchasing this book.
If you enjoy using it, we would
appreciate your review on Amazon.

Shadow Work: What is it?

Many people associate the word "shadow" with gloomy and dismal meanings. As a result, it's tempting to think of shadow work as a grim spiritual exercise involving our personalities' dark and sinister sides.

We are made up of both light and dark parts; the shadow is dark, but it's a part of our identity, and we can't be frightened of it.

The shadow is the unconscious and disowned aspects of our identities that the ego fails to perceive, acknowledge and embrace. It's any part of ourselves that isn't illuminated by the light of our awareness.

We are born entire and complete as children, yet that wholeness is fading. As a result of particular encounters with the individuals closest to us as children, the shadow emerges. Our caregivers convince us that specific characteristics of ourselves are positive and others are negative. The features that are perceived as unfavorable are rejected, resulting in the shadow.

How can your shadow affect you?

We repress the features that are disliked and emphasize the aspects that are acceptable when we rely on our caretakers for survival.

Imagine a sensitive eight-year-old boy. He is soft-hearted, and something makes him cry. "Stop sobbing like a little girl, be a man!" his father responds.

You must have heard or seen this kind of instance multiple times. Because his father feels that sobbing is wrong, he suppresses his son's feelings. As a result, the boy pushes his soft and sensitive side into the background and starts "playing tough." He has problems experiencing things as an adult and refuses to display his feelings, even when it is essential. He suffers in his relationships as a result of this, never allowing himself to be seen entirely.

Another example is a little girl who becomes enraged over something and begins to throw a tantrum. Her mother immediately orders her to "Stop it! Stop being such a jerk!" Every time she gets furious, her mother tells her to calm down and be a nice girl. The small girl grows up with the notion that getting angry is bad, and tries so hard not to become furious. She dissociates from her emotions over time, but this does not make them go away.

She grows up raised with the belief that she must constantly be in control. She later recognizes that she is having problems at work because others are pushing her buttons. She frequently feels as though she is going to burst and has no idea what to do. She recognizes that her anger is always present, manifesting itself in passive-aggressive ways and causing problems at work.

How to do shadow work?

So, how do you go about identifying your shadow? It all comes down to bringing the unconscious mind into our waking consciousness. Psychoanalytic thinkers saw this as crucial to preserving psychological well-being.

It's usually done using the "Socratic method" of inquiry and investigation. Asking objective questions that prompt critical thinking and re-examining past assumptions about ourselves is part of this process.

The concept is that a more objective entity (like a therapist) might assist in holding up an interpretative mirror to the aspects of ourselves that we find difficult to see and accept.

While this is usually done with the guidance of a therapist, you may start exploring your shadow on your own by evaluating your ideas, feelings, and assumptions. You'll find some prompts to assist you below. The elements of ourselves that have been pushed down to the unconscious — the portions that we're anxious about, embarrassed about, or frustrated with, and hence repress — are known as the "shadow self." The shadow self is founded on the idea that we bury those aspects of our personalities that we fear will not be received, accepted, or appreciated by others. Therefore, we keep them hidden in the "shadows." To put it another way, our shadow selves are the versions of ourselves that we don't exhibit to the rest of the world.

What exactly is shadow work? This is the discipline of accepting what is and releasing guilt and judgments so that we can be our authentic selves. The greatest happiness in life is the conviction that we are loved — loved for ourselves, or rather, loved in spite of ourselves.

Benefits you can reap from shadow exercises

The unfortunate fact is that the term "shadow work" brings up all kinds of evil and dark ideas for a lot of individuals. It's natural to think of shadow work as a gloomy spiritual activity because of our connections with the word.

Alternatively, it might be internal work involving solely the more profound negative or dark sides of ourselves. Or perhaps it merely traps you in a state of helplessness and anguish. Or you're worried that if you concentrate just on the darkness, all you'll get is more shadow. All of this, however, is not the case. So let's look at the potential advantages of shadow work.

1. Shadowing is a valuable tool. It's a tool in the same way that focusing on the good is. You can master that tool, just as you can any other device. Working in the shadows isn't a way of life. It isn't something that you experience. It isn't something that takes up all of your time. It's not the whole picture. It's a technique for becoming aware, stepping out of and altering destructive patterns, entering a more objective reality, moving into free will and conscious choice, and thus actively and consciously constructing your existence.

2. Shadow work makes you more aware of your surroundings and allows you to see things. It's learning what you don't know about. It is, in fact, necessary for being conscious, aware, and awakened. It places you directly in the middle of the truth — in fact, in realism. As a result, shadow work may provide practically any advantage that comes from perceiving the truth, having a more objective perspective, being aware, or being in reality.

3. It gives you a sense of power. Your power axis exists in reality, and you can't live in that reality until you're conscious of it. Shadow, on the other hand, denotes a lack of consciousness. It alludes to what you're not aware of, as well as what you've suppressed, rejected, denied, repudiated, and pushed out of your consciousness.

You have a choice when you are aware. This implies you'll be in a position of free will rather than determinism. For example, you may not realize that you continually end up getting in relationships with red flags until you undertake shadow work.

Your early life experiences taught you that love is when someone is suffering and miserable in a relationship but remains because they care so much about the other person. You are then in a position to select compatible persons with whom to form a relationship.

Some people are afraid that doing shadow work would make them suffer even more. However, this will only happen if you begin to see things as they are but are persuaded you either can't or won't alter them.

4. In the gloom, there's a lot of gold. Many individuals believe that the shadow is entirely negative and terrible. Actually, there is a lot that a person doesn't know that is wonderful and enjoyable. Also, there is a lot of pleasant and joyful information that we repress, deny, reject, disavow, and push away from consciousness.

Consider the possibility that you were artistic as a youngster. Consider the case that you were born with the desire to be an artist. However, you were born into a household that was preoccupied with academics and shunned artistic expression.

You may have suppressed, rejected, and denied your creative gift, as well as your purpose, in order to be closer to your family. Shadow work will undoubtedly lead to the rediscovery of your artistic skill as well as your life's purpose.

5. Shadow work results in self-introspection. You become more genuine as a result of it. It makes you realize who you are and what your particular reality is. The process of socialization and trauma that we all eventually go through causes us to fragment, among other things. Our personas are, at their core, phony.

Our personalities are essentially the parts of ourselves that we associate with in order to be secure and away from vulnerability in the particular surroundings and circumstances in which we were reared until we become awake and aware of ourselves. We repress, reject, deny, and abandon the qualities that make us vulnerable or cause us to be judged by others. They become subconscious as a result of this. They are buried outside of our awareness, and we are unaware that they exist, despite being visible to others. This implies that we are not who we believe we are.

Shadow work reveals who you indeed are and what you truly desire. It helps you become more self-aware. Without self-awareness, there is no way to live a happy life. To pick what is best for you, you must first understand and own yourself. The only way to achieve a life of pleasure, happiness, and fulfillment is to choose what is uniquely correct for you.

6. Shadow work is a great way to get out of a rut. You're only genuinely stuck if you have no idea what's going on. To begin solving problems and taking action, you must first understand what is going on. That is accomplished through shadow work.

Many individuals believe that working in the shadows renders them weak. It doesn't... it just forces them to acknowledge their limitations. You are witnessing your limitations and thus, by facing them, you are not them. You are no longer a part of them. If you choose to bring consciousness to impotence, it is no longer powerless by definition because you have added the frequency of free will to it. It makes you aware of patterns and cycles, causing you to disidentify with them and modify them so they don't reoccur and can be changed.

Individually and intergenerationally, people repeat patterns. As a result, the majority of individuals live in a deterministic manner. Over and over, they keep ending up with unavailable relationships. Addiction and abuse patterns and destructive fundamental beliefs are passed down from generation to generation. Over and over again, humanity repeats the same way. Shadow work breaks the cycle, breaks the chain, and allows you to modify these patterns so that you may select your beliefs, behaviors, and life experiences deliberately.

7. Integration is facilitated through shadow work. Peace is achieved via integration. It promotes internal integration, which leads to inner peace, and exterior integration, which leads to personal and global peace. It reverses the fragmentation process, which is the source of so much pain in both your life and the planet. It helps you get closer to your goals so you can achieve them.

8. To begin with, most people believe they know exactly what they want. They don't, though. For example, suppose you were reared in a conservative household that values marriage. In that case, you may believe that marriage is what you really desire, but the only reason you think you want it is for your family's approval.

For instance, we could aspire to be a lawyer, but in reality, we just care about money and social position, and we have a limited understanding of how to obtain these.

Shadow work reveals what you desire and why you want it. It also broadens the scope of what is feasible. Shadow work also shows what is getting in the way of your goals. It displays a level of resistance. Getting what you desire requires resolving such issues.

Consider this scenario: you have no idea why you can't lose weight no matter how hard you try. It's possible that shadow work will disclose that the portion of your consciousness in charge of your body has no desire to lose weight. It wants to be fat because it utilizes fat as a barrier against the world's dangers and as a replacement border. After all, you can't maintain your own goal.

It will be crucial to work with this section of your consciousness to develop a resolution if you want to lose weight. Every diet and fitness regimen will fail unless you do so.

9. Shadow work helps you recognize and overcome your trauma, which is the underlying issue causing the present patterns in your life that are causing you pain and suffering. This is, without a doubt, the most important thing on my list.

Trauma is a condition of the emotional and mental anguish brought on by unresolved suffering. You don't have to be mistreated or go through something that most people would consider a tragedy (such as war, sexual assault, or the death of a loved one) to be traumatized.

Birth in today's mainstream medical institutions is a stressful process. Weaning a baby is a challenging experience. Losing track of one's mother at a supermarket is unpleasant for a three-year-old.

Even the most exemplary parents on the planet will not be able to raise a child without causing them any harm. If we don't have a mechanism to address and thereby integrate the trauma we encounter as children, we will shape our lives and make decisions based on trauma.

10. We also have a propensity to forget about trauma or normalize it. Worse, since this is a mirror-based universe governed by what many refer to as 'the law of attraction,' this universe will continue to provide us additional opportunities to heal our traumas by placing us in similar situations over and over.

They also have a tendency to magnify or become wacky. For example, suppose we never dealt with the fact that our father abandoned us when we were four years old. In that case, we may decide that in order to avoid the agony of loss, we will become ultra-independent and never be linked to anybody again.

We will not only have intimacy troubles as adults as a result of this event, but we will also be forsaken by others. This trend will then worsen because if we are abandoned, we will use this fact to justify our initial decision to push others away before they have a chance to push us away, increasing the likelihood of their abandoning us.

Thus, it spirals into an ever-worsening vicious circle. We have the power to develop a solid, reliable relationship with others in our lives if we can become aware of and address the initial trauma, as well as the changes we made to ourselves as a result. Shadow work may also indicate that problems we believe were settled aren't, and that's why similar events keep recurring in our life.

11. Shadow work forces you to delve far below the surface of things. It connects you to the blueprint, or fundamental level of being, that lies underneath the surface of reality. Your knowledge, depth, capabilities, breadth, and expanse will all improve as a result of this.

It's similar to a two-dimensional human becoming three-dimensional. This allows you to see things that others can't and perform things that others aren't aware are possible. You get more robust as a result. This is why awakened individuals appear to be so much... more.

12. It allows you to be more aware of what you generate and manifest. Many teachers of the law of attraction and manifestation oversimplify this to the point of illiteracy. The power of concentration, purpose, and thinking is immense. The acts that one does to produce are also necessary.

However, in the time and effort it takes you to focus on one thing, your subconscious mind may focus on other things without you even realizing it. This is why an Olympic swimmer can swim and prepare dinner at the same time. Swimming is an entirely subconscious activity. Your conscious mind does not control the majority of your total personal vibration. And your point of attraction is your complete unique vibration.

In a cosmos governed by the law of attraction, this is huge. For example, if you sit down to say the affirmation "I am good enough," that idea will be contending with numerous other, far more ingrained and powerful frequencies, such as "I'm too overweight" and "No one truly wants me." People who believe they are good enough are always the worst types of people.

Your point of attraction is more complicated than whatever you consciously focus on and do. As a result, you have very little influence over what occurs in your life unless you conduct shadow work. Everything seems to happen TO you, and you have no idea why.

You may deliberately adjust and increase your point of attraction by being aware of the contents of your subconscious mind as well as what you don't know about the world and the cosmos.

And the more awake you are, the more mindful you are when it comes to what you think, say, choose, and do. It will seem like you have control over your life and understand why things happen the way they do.

This frees you from the feeling of being a victim. In the same line as creation, creativity is hampered by blocked energy and inauthenticity. Shadow work dissolves those barriers and resistances, allowing your creative potential to flow freely as the energy of conscious awareness passes through you. You become a much more creative person as a result of this.

13. Shadow work aids in the development of effective, healthy, pleasurable, and mindful relationships. Relationships are vital to one's survival. You have other persons with whom you share a connection. Every aspect of your life, including your profession, diet, hobbies, and body, has a relationship with you. As a result, the quality of your connections determines the quality of your life.

Doing shadow work will make it harder for someone to trigger you. As a result, your interpersonal dynamics will become more mature, healthier, and more functional due to your maturation. You could, for example, have a mysterious connection with your child. Shadow work might indicate that you despise tendencies in your kid that you have hidden, denied, or rejected in yourself, such as selfishness

Perhaps you've dismissed your own egoism, and you're giving your life to your husband and children. However, you despise the fact that you're doing so. As a result, you experience animosity towards your child whenever they act in their best interests. This realization may force you to reconsider your decision and begin doing things for yourself.

14. It improves your physical, mental, and emotional health and well-being. Being unaware is difficult and stressful. Denying, repressing, rejecting, disowning, and pushing things away, or attempting to keep a closet door shut while its contents are overflowing, is exhausting and unpleasant.

Simply put, suppression produces weariness and sickness. The health of all of those layers of you will substantially improve as you unleash the repressed energy and enable more of the significance of consciousness to flow through all of them. You'll have extra stamina. Shadow work also gives you a sense of security and power, making you feel on par with life and very much alive.

These are only a few of the advantages of shadowing. The more aware you are of your shadow, the more embodied you are as a conscious person. Without facing and exposing their darkness to the light of consciousness, no one has ever achieved enlightenment. It is now up to individuals to master this tool, which will lead to their liberty.

Get to the Root of your shadow

The ancient Greeks recognized the importance of honoring all aspects of the mind. As a result, these components were revered as gods and goddesses in their own right.

The Greeks recognized that ignoring a god or goddess would result in that god or goddess turning against you and destroying you. Any aspect of ourselves that we reject turns against us. The personal shadow represents a collection of these disowned aspects.

So here's the issue: Without our complete awareness, the shadow can act on its own. It's as if our conscious self switches to autopilot mode, leaving the unconscious in charge. We do things we wouldn't choose to do and then regret it afterward (if we catch it). We say things that we wouldn't usually say. Our facial expressions reveal feelings we aren't aware of.

Our relationships with our spouses, families, and friends will suffer if we remain unaware of the shadow, as will our professional connections and leadership abilities.

How to Recognize Your Own Shadow

Nothing exists in the inherent condition of separation and division. On the contrary, humans are wired for integration and wholeness. Therefore, the subconscious will constantly strive to capture your attention to integrate what's there.

It might be tough to recognize your own shadow, especially if you've pushed a tiny portion of yourself into the unconscious mind. Here are three techniques for detecting your shadow in action:

1. Make a projection

Many individuals blame their problems on others. They point out flaws in others when they detest something about themselves. We frequently project our shadows — repressed anger, remorse, shame, and other aspects of ourselves that we dislike — onto others. Then, we strike out at others because we don't like our own behavior.

Keep an eye on how you present yourself to the rest of the world. People, places, and things become mirrors that reflect who we indeed are while the universe attempts to make us whole again.

2. Reactions

A trigger is a recollection of a previous traumatic event. The surface occurrences that generate tension in our lives are messengers that allow us to become aware of something hidden deep inside us. Please pay attention to your triggers; they might readily reveal your wounds and your shadow. Try to recognize your emotional triggers before acting out rather than afterward.

3. Patterns

Patterns in our life that repeat themselves represent components of our shadow. Because the shadow reflects itself into your reality to be viewed and assimilated, patterns are representations of the shadow.

The shadow wishes for you to notice it. It aspires to be noticed and accepted. You'll uncover components of your shadow self inside these patterns that will continue to crop up in new settings until you're ready to look at them and stop the cycle.

Wound Mapping

Many of our troubles stem from our unwillingness to confront our troubling ideas and feelings. Our inner lives become divided when we avoid acknowledging areas that produce vulnerability. Instead of interpreting our discomfort as either good or bad, we may use the whole range of our human experiences in surprising ways if we turn to confront those thoughts and feelings.

What sets us off, what presses our buttons, might reveal stuff buried in our shadow that must be addressed.

HERE'S A FUN ACTIVITY TO TRY:

Everyday situations that irritate you or push your buttons might cause unintended consequences (feelings and behaviors) that are out of proportion to the event. These are one-of-a-kind to you. However, there is a belief going on in the middle (between the activating situation and your response).

This is the belief that we want to bring to light through coaching. So, give it a go...

Acknowledge your own activating events.
Recognize the activating events that have occurred in your life. Consider the things that happen in your life that truly get you moving. Is it getting stuck in traffic? Is it that your kids aren't doing their chores? Is there a project that has gone over budget? Make a mental note of how much these occurrences affect you.

Activating event 1:

Activating event 2:

Activating event 3:

Now think of the consequences of these actions:

What effect did they have on you?

What exactly did you do?

Now we'll take a step back and consider the following belief:
What was going through your mind?

Alternative interpretations are being challenged and created.
Is there a method to put your belief to the test? Is this, for example, a 100 percent accurate interpretation? What proof is there, and where is it? Make a list of any examples or evidence that contradicts your ideas. What evidence does the list support when you think about it?

You imagine other perspectives.
If you discover that your list is biased, you can go further and come up with other ways to interpret the incident. For example, what are the details you're missing? Is there anything else that might be impacting the situation?

Our shadow parts can be integrated by recognizing our triggers and allowing them to lead us to hidden beliefs. We may begin to overcome their hold on our lives and lessen their negative influence and disturbance once we understand them and how they operate.

Positive Quotes

ALL THE BEAUTY OF LIFE IS MADE UP OF LIGHT AND SHADOW.

IT IS ONLY THROUGH SHADOWS THAT ONE COMES TO KNOW THE LIGHT.

NEVER FEAR SHADOWS. THEY MEAN THERE'S A LIGHT SHINING SOMEWHERE NEARBY.

Shadow Work

Prompts

Date: _____

Which emotion makes you feel the most uneasy or
uncomfortable to sit with? Which one do you try
to avoid the most?

_____

_____

_____

_____

_____

_____

_____

_____

_____

_____

_____

_____

_____

Today I am grateful for:

_____

_____

Did I get triggered today? Describe what happended:

_____

_____

_____

_____

Date: _____

Think back to a scenario or situation where that emotion played out. What happened? How did you react initially? What other emotions played out alongside the one you tried to avoid?

_____

_____

_____

_____

_____

_____

_____

_____

_____

_____

Today I am grateful for:

_____

_____

Did I get triggered today? Describe what happended:

_____

_____

_____

Date: _____

What negative emotions are you most comfortable with? Do you cling to certain emotions on a day-to-day basis because they feel 'normal'?

_____
_____
_____
_____
_____
_____
_____
_____
_____
_____
_____
_____
_____

Today I am grateful for:

_____
_____

Did I get triggered today? Describe what happended:

_____
_____
_____
_____

Date: _____

Is your inner voice kind or critical? What things does it say to you on a typical day?

_____

_____

_____

_____

_____

_____

_____

_____

_____

_____

_____

Today I am grateful for:

_____

_____

Did I get triggered today? Describe what happended:

_____

_____

_____

_____

Date: _____

Is your inner voice truly yours? Whose voice could be influencing your inner voice (parents, partners, teachers, friends, etc.)? Would you say the things that the voice tells you to other people? If not, then those thoughts aren't your authentic voice. Instead, they're reflections of other people's beliefs you've internalized.

_____

_____

_____

_____

_____

_____

_____

_____

_____

Today I am grateful for:

_____

_____

Did I get triggered today? Describe what happended:

_____

_____

_____

_____

Date: _____

Look at your past. Who has or still does regularly downplay how you feel?

_____

_____

_____

_____

_____

_____

_____

_____

_____

_____

_____

Today I am grateful for:

_____

_____

Did I get triggered today? Describe what happended:

_____

_____

_____

_____

Date: _____

"I am easily influenced or swayed by the opinions and beliefs of others. As a result, I find it hard to assert my voice and figure out what is them versus me." Explore this statement.

_____

_____

_____

_____

_____

_____

_____

_____

_____

_____

_____

_____

Today I am grateful for:

_____

_____

Did I get triggered today? Describe what happended:

_____

_____

_____

_____

Date: _____

"I regularly downplay how I feel or what I'm thinking for the sake of others." Do you agree or disagree with this statement?

_____

_____

_____

_____

_____

_____

_____

_____

_____

_____

Today I am grateful for:

_____

_____

Did I get triggered today? Describe what happended:

_____

_____

_____

_____

Date: _____

Why do you let people who don't acknowledge your feelings stay in your life? Do you have a desire to keep their company? Or do you know that there's something you could be doing to make the relationship better?

_____
_____
_____
_____
_____
_____
_____
_____
_____
_____

Today I am grateful for:

_____
_____

Did I get triggered today? Describe what happended:

_____
_____
_____
_____

Date: _____

Do you value yourself and what you bring to the table?

_____

_____

_____

_____

_____

_____

_____

_____

_____

_____

_____

Today I am grateful for:

_____

_____

Did I get triggered today? Describe what happended:

_____

_____

_____

_____

Date: _____

How can you be kinder to yourself? In what
ways do you punish or sabotage yourself?

_____

_____

_____

_____

_____

_____

_____

_____

_____

_____

_____

_____

Today I am grateful for:

_____

_____

Did I get triggered today? Describe what happended:

_____

_____

_____

_____

Date: _____

How important are you to yourself?

_____
_____
_____
_____
_____
_____
_____
_____
_____
_____
_____

Today I am grateful for:

_____
_____

Did I get triggered today? Describe what happended:

_____
_____
_____
_____

Date: _____

Have you ever done something just to make
someone else feel proud of you? If so, who was it,
and why?

_____

_____

_____

_____

_____

_____

_____

_____

_____

_____

_____

_____

_____

Today I am grateful for:

_____

_____

Did I get triggered today? Describe what happended:

_____

_____

_____

Date: _____

Do you fully celebrate your achievements? Or is there a disconnect between your accomplishments and who you are as a person? Which one resonates more?

_____

_____

_____

_____

_____

_____

_____

_____

_____

_____

_____

Today I am grateful for:

_____

_____

Did I get triggered today? Describe what happended:

_____

_____

_____

_____

Date: _____

What is your biggest regret to date?

_____

_____

_____

_____

_____

_____

_____

_____

_____

_____

_____

_____

Today I am grateful for:

_____

_____

Did I get triggered today? Describe what happended:

_____

_____

_____

_____

Date: _____

Imagine you're coming to the end of your life. What is the biggest regret you fear having the most? How does that make you feel, and where does it sit within the body?

_____

_____

_____

_____

_____

_____

_____

_____

_____

_____

Today I am grateful for:

_____

_____

Did I get triggered today? Describe what happended:

_____

_____

_____

_____

Date: _____

Imagine your worst fear came true. How does that make you feel now about your life ahead?

_____

_____

_____

_____

_____

_____

_____

_____

_____

_____

_____

_____

_____

Today I am grateful for:

_____

_____

Did I get triggered today? Describe what happended:

_____

_____

_____

_____

Date: _____

Imagine your most wanted dream came true right now. How does that make you feel about your life ahead? Are there similar feelings and emotions tied to both your fears and successes?

_____

_____

_____

_____

_____

_____

_____

_____

_____

_____

_____

Today I am grateful for:

_____

_____

Did I get triggered today? Describe what happended:

_____

_____

_____

Date: _____

Do you feel you're only as good as your last achievement? If yes, why? If no, why not?

_____
_____
_____
_____
_____
_____
_____
_____
_____
_____
_____
_____
_____

Today I am grateful for:

_____
_____

Did I get triggered today? Describe what happended:

_____
_____
_____
_____

Date: _____

What do you think are your most undesirable traits
and characteristics? (This is NOT an opportunity to
put yourself down, but rather a chance to unearth
what you believe to be true about yourself. This
doesn't mean what you write is an accurate reflection
of yourself.)

_____

_____

_____

_____

_____

_____

_____

_____

_____

_____

Today I am grateful for:

_____

_____

Did I get triggered today? Describe what happended:

_____

_____

_____

_____

Date: _____

What image do you think other people have
of you?

_____
_____
_____
_____
_____
_____
_____
_____
_____
_____
_____
_____
_____
_____

Today I am grateful for:

_____
_____

Did I get triggered today? Describe what happended:

_____
_____
_____
_____

Date: _____

How would you like others to describe you? Is there a difference between your answer to this question and the previous one? How does that make you feel?

_____

_____

_____

_____

_____

_____

_____

_____

_____

_____

_____

Today I am grateful for:

_____

_____

Did I get triggered today? Describe what happended:

_____

_____

_____

_____

Date: _____

"If I could be anything in the world, I would be…"
Fill in the blank.

_____
_____
_____
_____
_____
_____
_____
_____
_____
_____
_____
_____
_____

Today I am grateful for:

_____
_____

Did I get triggered today? Describe what happended:

_____
_____
_____
_____

Date: _____

Why aren't you already doing the thing you mentioned in the above question? What's stopping you?

_____

_____

_____

_____

_____

_____

_____

_____

_____

_____

_____

Today I am grateful for:

_____

_____

Did I get triggered today? Describe what happended:

_____

_____

_____

_____

Date: _____

What is your definition of failure?

_____
_____
_____
_____
_____
_____
_____
_____
_____
_____
_____
_____

Today I am grateful for:

_____
_____

Did I get triggered today? Describe what happended:

_____
_____
_____
_____

Date: _____

"When I think back to a time that I failed, I feel..." Fill in the blank.

_____

_____

_____

_____

_____

_____

_____

_____

_____

_____

_____

Today I am grateful for:

_____

_____

Did I get triggered today? Describe what happended:

_____

_____

_____

_____

Date: _____

What is your definition of perfection? Is it attainable?

_____

_____

_____

_____

_____

_____

_____

_____

_____

_____

_____

_____

Today I am grateful for:

_____

_____

Did I get triggered today? Describe what happended:

_____

_____

_____

_____

Date: _____

Do you hold yourself to a higher standard than
you do others? If so, why?

_____

_____

_____

_____

_____

_____

_____

_____

_____

_____

Today I am grateful for:

_____

_____

Did I get triggered today? Describe what happended:

_____

_____

_____

_____

Date: _____

In what areas of your life do you feel inferior to others?

_____

_____

_____

_____

_____

_____

_____

_____

_____

_____

_____

Today I am grateful for:

_____

_____

Did I get triggered today? Describe what happended:

_____

_____

_____

_____

Date: _____

Have you ever sacrificed a part of yourself to fit in with others better?

_____

_____

_____

_____

_____

_____

_____

_____

_____

_____

_____

Today I am grateful for:

_____

_____

Did I get triggered today? Describe what happended:

_____

_____

_____

_____

Date: _____

Where are you playing small in your life?

_____
_____
_____
_____
_____
_____
_____
_____
_____
_____
_____
_____
_____
_____

Today I am grateful for:

_____
_____

Did I get triggered today? Describe what happended:

_____
_____
_____
_____

Date: _____

What narrative or stories do you tell yourself surrounding 'wanting more'?

_____
_____
_____
_____
_____
_____
_____
_____
_____
_____
_____
_____

Today I am grateful for:

_____
_____

Did I get triggered today? Describe what happended:

_____
_____
_____
_____

Date: _____

"If I could tell my younger self only one thing, it would be..." Fill in the blank.

_____

_____

_____

_____

_____

_____

_____

_____

_____

_____

_____

_____

Today I am grateful for:

_____

_____

Did I get triggered today? Describe what happended:

_____

_____

_____

_____

Date: _____

When have you felt abandoned by those
around you? Describe the situation and what
it made you think.

_____

_____

_____

_____

_____

_____

_____

_____

_____

_____

_____

Today I am grateful for:

_____

_____

Did I get triggered today? Describe what happended:

_____

_____

_____

_____

Date: _____

How do you show up for others in ways that you
don't show up for yourself?

_____

_____

_____

_____

_____

_____

_____

_____

_____

_____

_____

_____

Today I am grateful for:

_____

_____

Did I get triggered today? Describe what happended:

_____

_____

_____

_____

Date: _____

What do you need to forgive yourself for?

_____
_____
_____
_____
_____
_____
_____
_____
_____
_____
_____

Today I am grateful for:

_____
_____

Did I get triggered today? Describe what happended:

_____
_____
_____
_____

Date: _____

"I feel the need to keep myself hidden and small for the sake of others' feelings." Explore this statement.

_____

_____

_____

_____

_____

_____

_____

_____

_____

_____

_____

_____

_____

Today I am grateful for:

_____

_____

Did I get triggered today? Describe what happended:

_____

_____

_____

_____

Date: _____

"I've stayed in relationships (either platonic or romantic) that deep down I knew weren't good for me. Why did I do that?" Explore this statement and the feelings it brings up.

_____

_____

_____

_____

_____

_____

_____

_____

_____

_____

Today I am grateful for:

_____

_____

Did I get triggered today? Describe what happended:

_____

_____

_____

_____

Date: _____

"I am worthy of good things coming my
way." Do you agree or disagree, and why?

_____

_____

_____

_____

_____

_____

_____

_____

_____

_____

_____

Today I am grateful for:

_____

_____

Did I get triggered today? Describe what happended:

_____

_____

_____

_____

Date: _____

How would you feel and why if you were to live
the remaining years of your life as an exact repeat
of what has gone by? Where would you make
changes?

_____

_____

_____

_____

_____

_____

_____

_____

_____

_____

_____

Today I am grateful for:

_____

_____

Did I get triggered today? Describe what happended:

_____

_____

_____

_____

Date: _____

Describe the time when you felt the most alone.

_____
_____
_____
_____
_____
_____
_____
_____
_____
_____
_____
_____

Today I am grateful for:
_____
_____

Did I get triggered today? Describe what happended:
_____
_____
_____
_____

Date: _____

"In the past, I have let people take advantage of
me." Explore this statement.

_____

_____

_____

_____

_____

_____

_____

_____

_____

_____

Today I am grateful for:

_____

_____

Did I get triggered today? Describe what happended:

_____

_____

_____

_____

Date: _____

Does acknowledging that other people have taken advantage of you bring up any anger, resentment, or discomfort? If you could turn back the clock, what would you do differently?

_____
_____
_____
_____
_____
_____
_____
_____
_____
_____
_____
_____

Today I am grateful for:

_____
_____

Did I get triggered today? Describe what happended:

_____
_____
_____
_____

Date: _____

Where do you need to set better boundaries in your life?

_____
_____
_____
_____
_____
_____
_____
_____
_____
_____
_____
_____

Today I am grateful for:

_____
_____

Did I get triggered today? Describe what happended:

_____
_____
_____
_____

Date: _____

Did your parents always address and meet your needs as a child?

_____

_____

_____

_____

_____

_____

_____

_____

_____

_____

_____

_____

_____

Today I am grateful for:

_____

_____

Did I get triggered today? Describe what happended:

_____

_____

_____

_____

Date: _____

Did your teachers and school peers treat you with
the respect and love you deserved as a child?

_____

_____

_____

_____

_____

_____

_____

_____

_____

_____

_____

Today I am grateful for:

_____

Did I get triggered today? Describe what happended:

_____

_____

_____

Date: _____

Thinking back to a time in your childhood when you felt different or outcast, do you notice any similarities between that moment and how you go about your daily life now? Are there childhood fears appearing in your adult life?

_____

_____

_____

_____

_____

_____

_____

_____

_____

_____

Today I am grateful for:

_____

_____

Did I get triggered today? Describe what happended:

_____

_____

_____

_____

Date: _____

What makes you so angry that you don't tell
anyone and instead internalize and bury it?

_____

_____

_____

_____

_____

_____

_____

_____

_____

_____

_____

Today I am grateful for:

_____

_____

Did I get triggered today? Describe what happended:

_____

_____

_____

_____

Date: _____

What do you think about yourself when
people say they love you?

_____

_____

_____

_____

_____

_____

_____

_____

_____

_____

_____

_____

Today I am grateful for:

_____

_____

Did I get triggered today? Describe what happended:

_____

_____

_____

_____

Date: _____

Do you fear that other people may see your hidden anxiety or insecurity?

_____

_____

_____

_____

_____

_____

_____

_____

_____

_____

_____

Today I am grateful for:

_____

_____

Did I get triggered today? Describe what happended:

_____

_____

_____

_____

Notes

Notes

Notes

Notes

Notes

Notes

Notes

Notes

Notes

Notes

Printed in the USA
CPSIA information can be obtained
at www.ICGtesting.com
LVHW051824041123
762964LV00014B/10